THE ART OF TEACHING WITH INTEGRITY

GIVING CHILDREN A VOICE

ELAINE YOUNG

AUTHOR OF <u>I AM A BLADE OF GRASS</u> AND
<u>CREATING A HIGH INTEREST CLASSROOM</u>

authorHOUSE®

MT

AuthorHouse™
1663 Liberty Drive, Suite 200
Bloomington, IN 47403
www.authorhouse.com
Phone: 1-800-839-8640

This book is a work of non-fiction. Unless otherwise noted, the author
and the publisher make no explicit guarantees as to the accuracy of
the information contained in this book and in some cases, names of
people and places have been altered to protect their privacy.

First published by AuthorHouse 5/22/2008

ISBN: 978-1-4343-7891-0 (sc)

Printed in the United States of America
Bloomington, Indiana

This book is printed on acid-free paper.

2/18/09

The Art of Teaching with Integrity

A dreamer of dreams
great visions often start
with small raindrops

Dedication

To my granddaughters Alison and Jordan who motivate me to have the light shine in every child's eyes."

Chapter Synopsis for
The Art of Teaching with Integrity

Chapter I "Welcome to the Unexpected"

Describes the process of interest based learning that I developed in my classroom. I taught second grade for 30 years in many diverse communities from latch key children to migrant workers to affluent communities.

Chapter 2: "Recipes for Success"

Real recipes for classroom activities with inspirational ideas.

Chapter 3: "Winning Strategies for Change"

It will create a distinction in understanding change from a problem and solution; to a dilemma we are faced with and the opportunity we can create.

Chapter 4: "Elaine's Philosophy questions"

Identify our assumptions and continuing the dialogue for creating an interest based learning collaborative community.

Chapter 1

Welcome to the Unexpected

I have always wanted to make children feel good about themselves. I want to make them feel that they can learn, that they can succeed, that they can do anything. It seemed that if I could somehow touch the inside of each child and demonstrate his or her own special qualities, I would convince my students how important they are to me and to others. Then most of the battle would be won. *How* could I help them to see their own worth? It was from that question that the opportunity to develop my method of teaching came about.

Interest Based Learning is the process of giving children choices and power in determining the shape of their education, thereby teaching them skills invaluable to them in later life. Children are not generally involved in the design of their own education. Their education is, instead, created *for* them by the teachers and the larger public school system.

For politicians and the educational bureaucrats, reform is about standardized tests, what they call "New accountability." But while inexperienced non-professionals create myopic standards, we have an epidemic of violence in the schools. These same schools create children who cannot read, but can pass those tests. We are not including everybody in the dialogue -- not the teachers who have the experience, and, most importantly, not the children! My objective is to prove that when children design their own learning environments, based on their own interests, they are more willing to be responsible for the results and for themselves.

Although within the construct of Interest Based Learning students are responsible for shaping their education, there *is* a structure, however non-traditional. Children are not making decisions alone. Instead they are required to come to consensus together through teamwork and project development. IBL students *must* come to an agreement about how they will accomplish their goals and learn the skills necessary to pass required exams. The critical difference between Interest Based Learning and exam-based learning is that, because IBL students use the skills, knowledge, and information necessary to pass the tests in their projects, they won't forget them after the exam. I once had a student who said it this way: "IBL is a live learning experience." This structure is flexible, yet it requires the children to set goals and time frames for themselves while continuously identifying their accomplishments.

There is a pattern of collaboration between the teacher and the students. Through collaboration and teamwork, the children hold each other accountable for their contributions to the team project. The children also learn to make and take seriously the commitments that they have made to the teacher. Interest Based Learning instills more responsibility and accountability than test-based learning and in turn, this kind of discipline creates an invaluable sense of pride. The Random House Dictionary defines discipline as an "activity, exercise, or regiment that develops or improves a skill; training." This is the focus of the IBL classroom. The discipline of teamwork, solving problems, and consensus building is the necessary foundation for learning.

The IBL teacher, just as any other teacher, is still responsible for fulfilling the curriculum requirements and insuring that the children are prepared for exams. The students use the skills, knowledge, and information in their projects to pass the tests instead of using them in unassociated worksheets, and are required to identify them and discover how they apply to life each day. IBL children are not just learning for the sake of passing exams. They learn because they are inspired to learn. They want to know more. Their curiosity and interests are motivated. In the IBL collaborative learning environment we create a respectful, orderly, cooperative, and trusting classroom. The students create the rules to which they will adhere in order to support their group and the class as a whole.

This method of teaching is not very different from other methods in that the goal is to help the students succeed and see themselves as leaders. This method differs, however, from others in the way that this goal is accomplished. When children appreciate that their own ideas are heard, accepted, and put into action, they begin to *see* themselves as leaders, and consequently *act* like leaders. This is true not only of their experiences in the classroom, but also in their lives.

Leadership is the ability to bring about consensus among your peers. I have consistently found that young children absolutely *do* have the ability to have their own ideas and solutions, and to pursue them. They can listen, and hear the ideas of others, and adapt them to fit the needs of everyone. One example of how this worked in my classroom took place in one of my Kindergartens. I purposefully did not provide many classroom materials in order to teach them about problem solving and working together. The students began to argue with one another over the few supplies they had. I listened to their complaints and then they asked me what they should do? I kept asking them what the problem was. They finally agreed the real problem was "we don't know how to share."

I eventually asked them what their solution was. The Kindergartners decided to make a graph of the time and materials used by each student and then determine what was appropriate. Through this experience the kids discovered how math could be applied to life experiences and how graphs are used in the real world. Their interests now became a teaching tool and a research inquiry process.

Children need to solve problems related to real life experiences. This provides the opportunities for their voices and opinions to be heard. When the problem solving process is team based, children are able to identify their own and each others talents and abilities. These talents and abilities, such as artistic, musical, speaking, writing, interpersonal skills, just to name a few, are those to which Howard Gardner refers in his groundbreaking work <u>Multiple Intelligences</u>.

The goal of Multiple Intelligences Theory, as well as Interest-Based Learning, is to develop talents and abilities and help students reach vocational and avocational goals. Gardner's ideal school is based on the assumption that not all people have the same interests and abilities. Teachers identify and use the children's intelligences in class projects, and enable children to identify their own talents and abilities. At the same time the children recognize the abilities of fellow students and collaborate with them in the problem solving process. Through Interest Based Learning students practice the art of observing and questioning. This inquiry process becomes a life long habit.

An important aspect of IBL teaching is to practice the habit of asking the children what they think, how they feel, and what they need. When you truly listen, the children will ask you to be their partner in the inquiry process. The inquiry process doesn't have to wait until college; it can start in Kindergarten. It is important to be honest and be able to say,

"I don't know either, how can we find out?" Ask the children, we are all learners together.

Problem Solving

Problem solving requires using thinking skills. Thinking skills include observing, analyzing, comparing, classifying and summarizing. I wanted the children to do the thinking not just learn the words. We used them in all of our activities. I identified the skills as the children were using them. I used the words "summarize", "analyze", "compare" etc. when ever it applied to a "doing thinking" process. Children aren't waiting to grow up someday, they are already grown up so I treated them and spoke to them as I would adults. I wanted them to be aware of what they were doing and why.

Problem solving within Interest Based Learning can reveal and nurture mathematical abilities, which are far beyond the expectations of conventional schools. The signs in the hallways of many schools state rules like "Don't run in the hallway". I opened a dialog with my second graders, by asking what they could do if they won't run in the hallway? One child said, "Are you crazy Mrs. Young? What do you mean 'what will we do', we won't run." I replied, "I know that. What else can you do if you're not running?" They agreed that they could not skip, hop or jump. Then a child said that this is the year of the Olympics and there is a "fast walk" that is now part of the Olympics. "Can we do a fast walk?" I asked. We needed to figure out what a fast walk is for each member of the class. We did the math and marked off with tape the fast walk for each child. My fast walk made me too fast for the children, so I had to go to the end of the line. I saw this as asking the children to look at a problem they were faced with and identify the opportunity it presented to create a new learning experience, in this case related to math.

One day Joey got caught by the principal. The principal said "Joey, don't you see the sign? Don't run in the hallway." Joey responded, "You are only *assuming* that I'm running. Now look at the clock there. A fast walk is legal in the Olympics. This is my marker. Now watch me." "OK," said the principal, and guess who got to go to the principal's office - the teacher. I had not shared this opportunity to teach math with my principal, and he didn't view it as productive or relevant to the second grade curriculum. He would come to visit my classroom, which was set up like an exploratorium, and find me on the floor working with the children. After his visits he would leave me notes that said things like "I'll come back when you're really teaching."

By allowing children to use their abilities they begin to understand that they are trusted and heard by adults. They are able to see their own self-worth and recognize their own talents and abilities, as well as the talents and abilities of others. When more children begin to understand these things and develop their capacity for leadership, our world moves closer to being a community that works for everybody. They learn to speak, listen, and collaborate for a consensus; skills that world leaders continually seek to master.

Classroom

The nature of an Interest Based Learning classroom is much like that of the already well-known Collaborative Learning classrooms. The students and teacher all work together to learn the materials, and rather than using only a lecturing style, the teacher encourages the students to participate through discussion, group projects, and field learning.

Recently many people have been shying away from the idea of a collaborative learning environment, saying that it is "too free" or that it puts too much emphasis on socializing and not nearly enough on comprehension of basic skills and facts. This opinion has become popular as collaborative classrooms are becoming more prominent, and have in many cases been less than successful. After examining this process for some time, I have come to the conclusion that is it not the concept of allowing children to have a more active role in their education which is flawed. Rather it is the method of implementation that is creating the problem.

While I was teaching, I always met with the parents and children during the summer and invited them to help set up the classroom for the coming year. The students were encouraged to bring in personal items that were important to them, which might include rock collections, their favorite books, shells. We created different areas of interest: a science corner, a library corner, bulletin boards for displays, "private" reading corners, a discussion area with a couch and carpet. The children and parents designed the layout of the classroom, but the same basic elements were present each year. By starting over the summer, the inquiry process began before the school year officially started. It was also the first opportunity for the parents and children to see that they had choices, and that their opinions were important.

Developing Themes

The shape of the Interest-Based Learning curriculum is recreated every year around the interests of each new class. The teacher becomes a partner with the students by using their interests as a basis for mastering the curriculum. The school year begins with brainstorming sessions about our individual interests, and how they overlap. We would list questions about our interests and continue bringing in items to represent them. We identified resources of information, such as parents, books, and museums. We would brainstorm the children's ideas and put their words on a chart paper. I would ask them with whom they would like to form a team, and an example of a project that they could agree upon that would answer their questions. Teams began to form by making new connections with other students. A team is a group of individuals who create what I call a "new web of relationships." I did not assign teams; the children formed their own groups based on common interests.

It took about six to eight weeks for each team to see how they could connect their interests to the rest of the class. The next stage was to have the children come up with a connected theme for the year. Insects, roads and superstitions are examples of class themes with which I have worked. In this manner they, the students, determined their course of study.

The theme allowed the children to make new connections, not only within their projects, but also with each other. In other words, they formed a "new web of relationships." It also enabled the class to come up with community projects for the whole class.

One year a garbage theme developed after one child left a banana on our windowsill. As it began to rot it attracted fruit flies. The children became interested and wanted to know more about the fruit flies and what happens to garbage. The father of one of the students was a scientist who worked at SUNY (State University of New York) Purchase, so we arranged to visit the college lab. Some of the college students explained genetics and answered the children's questions about the fruit flies. The genetic information was sophisticated but the children made charts and continued their inquiry, which led to questions about what happens to the garbage. This was also an important exercise for the college students as it gave them an opportunity to practice and access their communication skills. They learned to present the information in a manner that was entertaining and accessible, and we were invited to visit again.

After our SUNY Purchase visit I made some inquiries and found out about the Croton Land Fill in Croton-on-Hudson, NY, where the garbage in Westchester County was sent at the time. We went on a trip to the landfill and the children learned about sanitation workers and the hard work they had to do to collect the garbage. They found out about the landfills, the beginnings of recycling plants, and the barges that took the garbage out to sea. Long before recycling was common practice, the children "invented" separating the broken bottles from the other kinds of garbage, like the rotting banana that would eventually decompose.

Eventually the trips and visitors and literature come together and the children could relate individual work to the class theme. They kept identifying their own and each other's talents and abilities. I read aloud every day, choosing children's literature related to the interests of the class. When we choose a theme, we would also choose a book that the children all loved, one that I had read aloud. I would ask them if they would like to turn it into a play or a musical or a drama. They would re-tell the story in their own words. Parents would type it for them, and they produced a performance for the whole school. Parents would help with costumes, the art teacher with scenery, and the music teacher with original songs. Today one of the children who helped her mother make the costumes for *The Lion, the Witch and the Wardrobe* is now a costume designer in Los Angeles. Another child who helped write the play is now an independent film maker and is writing the scripts for her own work. A former kindergarten student is an accomplished photographer. The children learned what they loved, and loved what they learned, and eventually took their interests and passion and used it in their future careers. In some way it was integrated. Of course they did not all discover their career paths in elementary school, but they all began to explore the possibilities their interests could present.

By allowing the children choices and power in determining the shape of their education, they are taught skills which will be invaluable to them in later life. They can be held more accountable for their academic progress, and will become used to being held to this kind of standard. They will learn how to be leaders, able to discuss and come to consensus with their peers. Students quickly become acquainted with the abilities associated with planning and organizing. They will be more equipped with the skills of collaboration and teamwork, both of which have become valuable commodities in today's job market. Perhaps most importantly, children will be ingrained with a lifelong love for learning.

When children solve problems related to their experiences, it demonstrates that all the choices they make in life come from the decision making process. They are constantly reflecting, as we did everyday in our classroom during "acknowledgment time" upon what we had accomplished both personally and as team members. We ended each day with "we acknowledge," or "we appreciate," time. It was a time when we could acknowledge individual and group accomplishments, and ask others to acknowledge us for what we had achieved that day. We learned to recognize that we are responsible for the results of the choices we made. We could choose what we had accomplished or we could decide to make a new path or direction and continue with our project. A project was only complete if everyone agreed that it was. The children could identify the choices they had made. As Ben, a former second grader, said, "this is a live learning experience."

Children quickly learn that freedom, and the choices that come with it, are interdependent with responsibility. When their exploration leads to a void in their education, the teacher steps in to bridge the gap. Students then master the curriculum requirements and proceed with their projects having acquired the necessary skills. One example of this took place twenty years ago in one of my second grade classrooms. A child brought in a hornet's nest and we became interested in insects. As a result, a parent came in to tell us about the dangers of the insecticide known as sevin.

When the kids became interested in researching the use of insecticides in the environment and found a newspaper article about how insecticide sevin was being used by the parks department in a Long Island community. They became concerned about the effects of the insecticide upon people as well as insects. They asked me "What should we do?"

In reply I asked them what would they like to do. They responded by saying that "we know about insects and they are in the cocoon stage now. We would like to go out there, climb the trees and pick the cocoons off the trees ourselves," thereby making the use of insecticides unnecessary. I then invited them to write a letter to the head of the parks department in Long Island and make that request.

They received a return letter that took their suggestion seriously, but which basically said we already bought sevin and we have to use it. The children would not quit. They asked me "who was the boss of the bosses" and I told them it was the then Governor Cuomo. They did not know how to communicate the essence of what the head of the parks department had to say without using their own judgments. They decided to use his exact words and underline it or put a happy face around it. I then asked them what they would call the underlining or the happy faces and they came up with the word "Googleflex."

I now had the opportunity to teach language art skills to the classroom. I told them that what they were talking about were quotation marks. I asked the children to check the newspapers with their parents to check for googleflexes/quotation marks. About a week later Amy came in and said "I don't understand Mrs. Young, here are the googleflexes, and here are some dots inside in front of the words. Are those the bad words they left out?" You can have a sense of humor and fun when you teach the skills. I still look at those dots and think "Are they the bad words they left out?"

Building Self-Esteem Through Non-Judgmental Listening

Building self-esteem and confidence is rooted in letting people know that they are being heard. When teachers and other adults practice non-judgmental listening, the result is full self-expression by the children. I watched this happen in my classroom year after year. One student, Tommy, brought in a paper bag to our morning meeting. When he pulled out the frog he had just squeezed to death, the other children looked at me, as I had not said anything about the frog. In the silence another student, Amy, went up to Tommy and said, "We like *you*, but *that* is disgusting." She expressed her feeling of disgust, and distinguished it from how she felt about him personally. When children can be fully self-expressed, they are free to tell the truth as it is for them. I could then ask the children what we should do with the frog. They choose to have me find someone to dissect it so that they could learn more about frogs.

By welcoming the unexpected, in this case a dead frog, we began an in-depth inquiry process about frogs and natural environments. This happened through non-judgmental listening. When children know that they will not be judged by what they say or do, they will want to become part of the team, and they can then hear someone else's opinion. By creating a true dialog, as distinguished from a discussion or a debate, children feel free to express their ideas and opinions. They can say, "I don't like that," as Amy did, and it's not taken personally. This is an important part of team building. It allows the children to reflect on what they have said and done, and how their actions affected others. We begin to value and appreciate each other when we allow full self-expression and provide the opportunity to ask the children what they think and what they need, and truly listen to their responses.

When I brought former students back to comment on the lasting impact of our class, they said, "We knew what it was like to be fully self-expressed. We knew when we were heard and when we better shut-up." Sometimes it happened again for them in high school, but more often not until college. Parents and children were part of every meeting, equal participants in projects, lunch, interests; every day was like a family day. I envision every school having a "we appreciate" bulletin board. Before the parents come into a classroom, they write an accomplishment for their child and the teacher.

Mentorship

One of the great misconceptions about collaborative learning methods is that a teacher in such an environment is acting only as a facilitator. This implies that a collaborative learning teacher does not impart knowledge to the students, and that students are instead left to their own devices in the vague hope that they will teach themselves. In reality, a teacher in a collaborative learning classroom actually has more demands placed on her than in a lecture style classroom. The idea behind Interest Based Learning is that students will, through discussion and problem solving, come to understand the concepts that they are required to by the curriculum. In order for this to happen, the teacher cannot simply allow the students to meander aimlessly through a discussion, but must be able to ask questions that will spark productive discussions. The teacher leads students through the tough thinking that will cause them to make new connections and fully understand the concepts at hand.

For a teacher to be able to do this, she must know exactly what the curriculum requires of the students. Her challenge is to find a way for the children to identify the skills, knowledge and information they are using and to see that they expand them through to real life experiences to meet the required standards. This method therefore requires that adults be willing to work *alongside* children in education. Students and teachers begin to communicate on a new level, talking and discussing with one another. Students *want* to be involved with each other, teachers, parents, and the community in solving problems. A new web of relationships and communications is formed, creating an ongoing partnership for growth and learning.

The teacher is an example for the students as well as for the parents. The role of the teacher is being a mentor for listening and respecting one another, the parents also can model this role. Children learn to listen because they are learning what it is to be listened to and heard. Parents will therefore benefit from this as children will be mentors for their parents. They will practice the habit of listening. Also, because parents support the students' projects by identifying resources as well as contributing their own talents and abilities to team projects, they are more closely involved in their child's education. The parents ideas, talents, and abilities are then equally valued and utilized.

This type of education will require more dedication from teachers and will be more fulfilling for them. Teachers are not being compensated with money but they will be compensated with satisfaction in producing successful results for the students and for themselves. Because teachers and students are both acknowledged for their accomplishments, they will find themselves working in a more fully self-expressed environment. Teachers would need to be retrained but this would be a group project involving the entire school and the community. Reflection and self-evaluation will become a routine practice.

As I was willing to be at the same point of discovery as the children, I often said, "I don't know either, how can we find out?" My questions became an equal part of the children's questions, they were included in the children's question list. When we listed the questions and sent letters to the parents, mine were included, and we invited the parents to add their questions as well. This led to creating a sense of family, all our voices were heard. The parents became part of the research teams, and participating in the editing process, typing, etc. Their willingness to actively participate enabled the parents to involve their children in other family issues; what they thought and how they could help solve problems. Children could help decide who could help clean, watch brothers and sisters, shop for food, make shopping lists, etc.

The goal of full self-expression meant the adults as well as the children. Problem solving was the point. Observing the choices parents and children made deepened the relationships. The documentation evolved into yearlong projects ("The Scottish Times," "A Look at Insects"). Documentation was a collaborative effort. We saw that we needed each other. We continued to value and appreciate each other's multiple intelligences/talents and abilities. It cannot be done alone. The school secretary helped us with the plays, performances, writing the scripts, and making the books. Each year, theme publications as well as performances demonstrated our talents, abilities and skills, used and learned. We reflected with the parents what we learned and what we were still interested in, continuing research throughout our lives.

Each year I had to get the list of the parents before school started so that I could call them. The school did not want to give out this information because the principal might get calls to switch a student. The school secretary was supportive and I got the list anyway. I planned to call the parents to set up a meeting in my home, as the school was not open and available in the summer time. I called Joey's mom and introduced myself and said "I am going to be Joey's teacher next year and I am calling to get acquainted and find out what Joey's interested in." Her response was "School is not in session yet, he's not in trouble is he? You haven't heard his reputation have you?" I said no, I wanted to invite her and Joey and the other parents and children to my home so that we could talk about our interests, expectations and questions. I told her I would be meeting with the librarian and we would be looking for children's books related to the interests of the class. I would be reading aloud every day and I wanted to invite both the parents and the students to participate in this process. We met in my home, where my basement was set up like a classroom.

Once you start creating a relationship with the parents and children, you cannot deepen that relationship enough. It takes availability for phone calls and visits to the home for parents to know you really want them involved. This is the beginning of a true dialog where the parents trust that you want to hear their voices and concerns also.

New Standards

The problem illiteracy can present is lessened in an Interest-Based Learning classroom. Intensive research requires reading newspapers, books, articles, and other materials related to the children's interests and project development. Communication is enhanced because the students are required to share, summarize, and analyze their materials for the other groups. Students will not be pressured to learn how to read but instead will be motivated by their own interest in the research. The students must identify the skills as they are using them in their projects. Students are more prepared for tests because they become so accustomed to using the process of solving problems.

In order for Interest-Based Learning to be effective, the teacher must be familiar with the curriculum standards. When I was teaching curriculum standards were called "Scope and Sequence." I can still tell you about the skills that were required, they were very similar to the skills identified in today's "new standards" but phrased differently. I would review the standards with the parents, and they became partners with the children and me in identifying the skills, knowledge and information the children were using in their projects every day. The children reflected on what skills they were using on their projects and how they applied to life, and why they needed them.

When the children made a chart of how long each child used a resource from the writing center, they saw how graphing helped them identify individual and group use of resources. At this point I introduced the new math standards and we used the math book to look up other examples. Then the students made up their own math problems and we created our own textbook based on our group projects. By teaching math in this way, I did graphing with my kindergarten class, and percentages with my second graders.

Summary

Much of the difficulty behind any school reform seems to have been that many teachers feel that in order to adopt one method, they must throw away everything they used before. To do this is to throw the baby out with the bath water. Change is an evolving, adaptive process, *not* the creation of one formula for change. Reform is about building a model that can then be adapted to fit any need. If a teacher likes the idea of a collaborative learning classroom, but finds that she can be more effective by integrating the new method with a more traditional one, she should be given that freedom.

In the past, reform has consisted of the same ideas being recycled under different names, and then discarded. Every reform measure has been all or nothing; there has been no sense that perhaps certain methods should be tried in conjunction with one another. Teachers have not been able to study and decide for themselves what methods would work best for their own teaching styles and their students' needs. Most significantly, no substantial survey of the students themselves have been taken, asking them what they feel they need in order to perform better.

Overall it is important that one weighs the benefits and the burdens of Interest-Based Learning. Yes, there are many important concerns in regard to this type of educational method, but when one examines the positive aspects of this type of educational system there can be no question of the advantages it holds. The children are defining their own interests through their work and they are learning what it is to actually enjoy learning. When children are only taught that learning is something they have to do they do not see the importance of it or the connection it has to our daily lives. Through practicing the skills necessary for group projects and research the students know what it is to enjoy themselves and make the connection between those skills and everyday life. Children should not have to wait until they are adults to decide their interests, it should start the minute they learn how to speak and voice their opinions. That is the whole point of this type of education, that the children's voices be heard.

What it comes down to is that no reform effort has made a real, *lasting* change. I truly believe that the reason for this is that the children have not been involved. There has always been a fear of allowing children to have any kind of freedom in what or how they learn. In part, this stems from the fact that adults seem to think that children are not capable of decision making. It also seems to come from a fear that by giving freedom to children, adults will lose control. This does not necessarily have to be so.

Winning Strategies for Change

"Learn what you love, love what you learn: Clarifying Interest Based Learning in the classroom and the world." (Winning strategies for change)

Ways to Practice the Concept

We left off last chapter with the Winning Strategies for Change:

1. **Seize the opportunity that change can bring.**
2. **Don't be afraid to risk.**
3. **It can't be done alone. We need each other.**
4. **It takes time. Be persistent.**

In our rapidly changing world these strategies are invaluable to any one who finds themselves lost in the flood of new ideas and remedies. This is especially true of educators, who are constantly barraged with new "solutions" to the problems we face in schools today and made to follow those "solutions" to the letter, for better or for worse. For our purposes here, these educators are the people we will be dealing with and my intent is to help them meet whatever new standards are set forth, without compromising their integrity as a teacher who wants the children to learn and not just pass the tests.

1. Seize the opportunity that change can bring.

Change is going to continue to happen all around you and if you are not willing to look at the positive possibilities that arise out of it, you will get stuck where you are and disgruntled at the stagnancy of it all. You will feel you don't have a choice, but you do. Choice lies in every action. Do not get bogged down in the fact that you have to change, choose to change for the better.

When you chose teaching as a career you were motivated to make a difference in children's lives. You had a commitment and a vision about how to accomplish your goal. You need to get back in touch with that motivation and be willing to share it with your colleagues and administrators regardless of how you think they may react. Together you can observe and question the opportunities that change can bring.

2. Don't be afraid to risk.

This may not be an easy thing for you to do. It definitely wasn't easy for me because I was not running my classroom in a traditional style. To make change work we often have to go out on a limb. My motivation and commitment, as I said before, was to get children involved in the design of their own education, to inspire them to love to learn. It was a risk to ask the children how they wanted to go about this and a risk to tell my principal that this is what I intended to do but in the end I did both successfully. If you are committed to the outcome, risks come easier; you're willing to do different things, not just do things a little differently.

3. It can't be done alone. We need each other.

Change does not exist in a vacuum. One cannot simply do their own thing without suffering the ramifications of his or her actions. I learned this the hard way when I was teaching. Some administrators didn't like my method and said things like, "I know what works so do it my way." Others, to their credit, created communities that shared and worked together towards a common goal, were willing to try new things. These individuals were models towards a way of thinking. They allowed me to interact with them as people instead of titles, something few had allowed me to do before then. This type of open communication is imperative to any successful venture into the Interest-Based Learning method or similar types of collaborative teaching. It helps to create a support structure that will be there in success and defeat, one that will set common goals and be committed and responsible to ensure that they happen.

4. It takes time. Be persistent.

One should not expect to successfully accomplish his or her goals over night. At the same time one should not expect to accomplish one's goals without working towards them. It takes a strong commitment to stay the course. Reflecting, evaluating, and acknowledging your accomplishments is a motivation for being persistent, and persistence is what allows us to succeed in time. If you really want it, don't quit. In the end you'll find that despite all the hurdles you had to overcome, the path was a pleasure to travel. Your project is complete when you know it's complete. Only then can you move on to the next stage.

Introduction for Philosophy Questions

We are all philosophers. We spend our lives thinking about the world in which we live, trying to make sense of it all. We construct opinions, form beliefs and view the world in the best way we see fit. Children are our young philosophers, just as adults view the world with a seasoned eye, children view it with one that is fresh, new and inventive. They puzzle over the world and are fascinated with the complexities that they find, just as adults do. Sadly, it seems that no one is concerned with what children have to say. Their voice is not heard when we decide what will be taught and how it will be presented. Children must be given the opportunity to share their vision with the world. By introducing children at a young age to the discipline of philosophy, we are opening them up to the world of the unknown and the interpretive.

Encouraging children to think for themselves will allow them a personalized learning experience. They will receive and understand information, interpret it, and make it meaningful to themselves. After this is done, adults and children will carry a coherent dialogue, sharing their interpretations with each other. Children and adults will deepen their relationship, stressing the importance of empathy and understanding. Encouraging children to speak their mind will not only improve their critical thinking skills, it will also improve their self-confidence. Kids need to understand that what they feel and say will make a difference in the world around them, that their beliefs hold value outside of themselves. By viewing the world from varying perspectives, we can come to better understand our own perception of the world, and grow to be more tolerant and patient with other people's beliefs.

Elaine's Philosophy Questions

"What have schools done to bring the freedom of choices for students and adults?"

"What can educators and parents do to realize we are totally responsible for everything we do?"

"How can we recognize how our unconscious reactions affect our feelings and actions?"

"How can education evolve into a discovery method determined by the students questions?"

"How can we find the truths that are meaningful to the individual's life?"

"What are the questions we should be asking for the answers that we have?"

"Are people's actions the result of instinct or reason?"

"Everyone one of us is a unique individual. How can we discover that uniqueness?"

"How can we take care of our children like some people take care of their gardens?"

"What rights are everybody entitled to and does that include the children?"

"How has your experience affected your mind and the way you see education?"

"How can we question and understand each others views and interpretations and who they are?"

"How can we not jump to conclusions?"

"Is it your reason or your feelings that get you happy or unhappy?"

"Can you construct your own philosophy?"

Elaine's educational philosophy is "Dare we ask the children" and involve them in all school change issues. Young children can be involved in an inquiry process that is project team and theme based. Give children a voice based on their interests.

Chapter 2

Little Voices, Big Ideas

On the following pages, you will see the product of a collaboration between a second grader named Caleb, myself, and some well known philosophers, people of notable fame and others. Caleb came to me through my radio show, *The Westchester Classroom*, on WVOX. He impressed me right away as he answered my first question, "What is your favorite thing to do?" with: "Well, Elaine, I love to learn."

How can we, as educators, motivate and inspire more kids to be like Caleb, I wondered? We started working together on an idea that came to me out of my own love of books and learning. I had always wondered how children would respond to esoteric statements, or even simple statements made by some of the great minds of our time and throughout history. Caleb and I sat down with some of the words that have inspired me, and many others, to see.

Caleb's candid responses, interpretations, examples and illustrations of these interpretations are collected in this book.

This section of the book is meant to be used as a workbook. I envision teacher's using Caleb's words to inspire their students to think about some of these famous words and come up with their own interpretations, examples and illustrations.

Interpreting, in general, relates to real life problems. Children must employ thinking skills, modify their understanding, generate creative solutions, draw conclusions, observe and describe, analyze, compare and contrast, understand each other's interpretations. Each quote can be dated to a time, a place, an event, a luminary persona, sparking a curiosity in history, science, or mathematics, and formulating new questions about and within these subject areas. Then they can go on to choose resources to further their investigations.

All of these types of critical thinking skills are exactly what the new state standards around the country demand from our students. By using these quotes, I hope a dialogue can begin in classrooms around the country about just what it is that things mean. So much is open to interpretation. But each child will bring their own interpretation to the table. This will enable teachers to involve the children in their own educational development and enrich their love of learning.

Until now, no workbook has attempted to give children's voices credibility and authenticity. Teacher's can use this book to encourage children to be fully self-expressed; to say what they think, how they feel, and what they need. It will empower children to realize that everyone has different ideas, and will teach them how to value and appreciate other's values, opinions and thoughts. This may be the one motivating factor to touch parents, students and teachers to want to learn and to communicate with one another. This is critical as we try to improve our society, one in which we are constantly judged, and where to be understanding and accepting of other's is like speaking a foreign language.

A young woman studying to become a teacher shared her feelings about this book with me, saying: "Right now in education, there is not enough emphasis on a child's interpretation of literature beyond their reading level. This is a way to make them think more critically."

As parents and teachers get to intimately know the children, this workbook offers practical classroom exercises to enhance the dialogue.

Caleb's Interpretations:

Thoreau "For mutual understanding is love's essence, for it is only by trying to understand others that we can have our own hearts understood."

Caleb's Interpretation:

"It's good to understand people, and yourself. Because it's a way of communicating. If I understand you and you understand me, we understand each other, we get to know each other and we get to love each other. Because when you know a lot of things about people which you like, it gives you time to look straight into their heart and see if it's a kind heart. If it's a kind heart, it's probably true that you'll like each other and liking leads to loving."

<u>Caleb's Example:</u>

"I just graduated from college with a girl. She begins to talk to me and I begin to understand her. I begin to like her and then love her. Then we get married."

Thoreau "For mutual understanding is love's essence, for it is only by trying to understand others that we can have our own hearts understood."

Your Interpretation:

<u>Your Example:</u>

27

Abraham Lincoln-"Most folks are about as happy as they make up their minds to be."

Caleb's Interpretation:

When a person is happy, he or she makes up their minds to be happy.

Caleb's Example:

I'm sad and I want to be happy. How I make up my mind is by picturing colors in my head.

Illustration:

Abraham Lincoln-"Most folks are about as happy as they make up their minds to be."

Your Interpretation:

Your Example:

Illustration:

Anonymous: "A lie can be halfway round the world before the truth gets its pants on."

Caleb's Interpretation:
Lies can pass around very quickly before the truth is heard.

Caleb's Example:
I'm in class. David says I love Mackenzie. That's a whopper of a lie. David tells people. Everyone thinks it's true until I say, "It's not true!"

Illustration:

Anonymous: "A lie can be halfway round the world before the truth gets its pants on."

Your Interpretation:

Your Example:

Illustration:

Charles Darwin- "Who should imagine that a great painter appreciates the sunset less than a silly boy or a sentimental school girl."

Caleb's Interpretation:

An artist sees a picture as many colors together making one design. Artists see objects differently than other people do.

Caleb's Example:

An artist looks at the reflection on a coffee machine. He sees all the colors are joining to make one design. Then a silly boy and a sentimental girl come in and they say "That's just a regular reflection. Nothing interesting." The girl and the boy didn't think the reflection was special because they didn't take time to see the colors joining together to make one design.

<u>Illustration:</u>

Charles Darwin-"Who should imagine that a great painter appreciates the sunset less than a silly boy or a sentimental school girl."

Your Interpretation:

<u>Your Example:</u>

<u>Illustration:</u>

Albert Einstein: "You should strive to make things as simple as possible but no simpler."

Caleb's interpretation:

You should try to make things as easy as you can, but not too easy. Maybe if it's too easy, nobody would understand it and know what you're actually trying to say.

Caleb's example:

Mom said to write an answer to a question that was simple, but not too simple, otherwise nobody would understand it.

Illustration:

Albert Einstein: "You should strive to make things as simple as possible but no simpler."

Your Interpretation:

Your Example:

Illustration:

John Lennon: "You may say I'm a dreamer, but I'm not the only one."

Caleb's Interpretation:
"A person can dream about anything they want, but they're not the only one's who can dream."

Caleb's Example:
I never thought young kids were PTA material. But I am, even though I'm only seven.

Illustration:

John Lennon: "You may say I'm a dreamer, but I'm not the only one."

Your Interpretation:

Your Example:

Illustration:

Sarah Fleming, Author of <u>In Code: A Young Woman's Mathematical Journey</u>- "A computer can solve the problem, but it can't explain why only eight are found."

Caleb's interpretation:

The computer wouldn't give you how it thinks it got the answer, and you would explain how you got the answer.

Caleb's example:

My teacher gives me a problem. I go onto the computer and it fives me 8 answers, but it doesn't explain how it got the answers. The next day my teacher fives me the same question and tells me to find the answer myself and explain how I got it. Then I end up writing extremely long explanations of how I thought to find the answer.

Illustration:

Sarah Fleming, Author of <u>In Code: A Young Woman's Mathematical Journey</u>- "A computer can solve the problem, but it can't explain why only eight are found."

Your Interpretation:

<u>Your Example:</u>

<u>Illustration:</u>

Other Voices

Abraham Lincoln-"Most folks are about as happy as they make up their minds to be."

<u>Zoe Parker's interpretation (11 yrs. Old)</u>:
When people are upset, they feel sorry for themselves (which they decide to do.) Instead of feeling sorry for yourself, it would be easier and more worthwhile to decide you're happy. Example: On a rainy day, instead of focusing on the rain, decide that you can be doing more worthwhile things inside, like reading.

<u>Adult response/interpretation</u>:
This brings to mind a famous aphorism my sixth grade teacher once quoted, which I have never forgotten: When life gives you lemons, make lemonade!

Anonymous: "A lie can be halfway round the world before the truth gets its pants on."

<u>Maddy Kolker's interpretation (11 yrs. Old)</u>:
People will believe anything someone tells them before they have any information. Example: A rumor went around my school that an eighth grader committed suicide and none of it was true.

<u>Adult response</u>:
A sin has many tools. A lie is the handle that fits them all.

John Dewey: "The real alternative to settling questions is not mental confusion but the development of the spirit of curiosity that will keep the student in an attitude of inquiry and of search for new light."

<u>Justin Cummings' interpretation (10 yrs. old)</u>:

When you're answering questions you don't have to get all confused. So the development of a person is in their curiosity, which will keep their attitude in search of new things. Example: Me and my friend were playing darts once and he was saying, "I give up. I can't play darts." And then he threw the dart with his head turned away from the target in frustration, and hit the bullseye.

<u>Glossary:</u>

Attitude

Caleb's definition-how a person is feeling.

Justin's definition-the way a person acts.

Webster's New World College Dictionary Fourth Edition definition-the position or posture assumed by the body in connection with an action, feeling, mood, etc.

Dream

Caleb's definition-when someone thinks without someone thinking with the person.

Webster's New World College Dictionary Fourth Edition definition-to imagine as possible; fancy; suppose.

Explain

Caleb's definition-to show how you found the answer to a problem or a question.

Webster's New World College Dictionary Fourth Edition definition-to make clear, plain, or understandable. To give the meaning or interpretation of; expound.

Sunset

Caleb's definition-the sun setting on the horizon.

Webster's New World College Dictionary Fourth Edition definition-the daily disappearance of the sun below the western horizon.

Understanding

Caleb's definition-when you get to know someone.

Webster's New World College Dictionary Fourth Edition definition-the mental quality, act, or state of a person who understands; comprehension, knowledge, discernment, sympathetic awareness, etc.

Define your own interpretations! Your voice matters too. Adults are somebody's children also.

The Cockamamie Things People Say about Education And Their Interpretations

Many times in life people are forced to listen to others even when they do not agree with what is being said. This is especially true within the education system. All people, including teachers, parents, administrators, and students need to be more conscious of the consequences before speaking. By showing that there are many miscommunications and situations that can be interpreted differently, changes within education can be made. These changes will include enhanced relationships, increased compassion, and enabling everyone to express their feelings without fear of judgment. It must be noted that the negative conversations are far easier to remember than the positive ones. This chapter's goal is to provide readers with an understanding that conversations can be misunderstood, and there are many ways to reinterpret them, causing a more positive environment.

High School Students

Example:

A ninth grader could not see the blackboard during her lesson because her eyesight was bad and asked a friend sitting next to her what it said. The teacher reprimanded her for talking during class. When the student told the teacher why she was talking, the teacher responded, "You cannot see the board because you are talking too much."

Student's Interpretation: She felt that the teacher should have told her to ask her rather than speaking to the other students. She was also embarrassed because the teacher failed to think about how she was making the student look in front of her other peers. The student also feels that the teachers need to put themselves in the students' positions before she speaks next time to avoid miscommunications.

Example:

A high school Math teacher taught the lesson in a way that the student did not understand. The student did not ask for help until the review for the test. When asking the teacher privately for help, the teacher told her that she should have known the material by now.

Student's Interpretation: The teacher had made her feel stupid. Though she was discouraged from asking questions in this class, it did not stop her from asking other teachers for help. The student also felt that the teacher should have explained this because it was a test review. She felt that this was an appropriate time for questions. Though the student admits to talking a lot during class, she believes that she did not understand the material for other reasons because she was paying attention during the lesson.

Example: Teacher said, "I'd rather slit my wrists than teach this class."

Student's Interpretation: The student admits the class did not behave well, however could not help to wonder what they had done to warrant a reaction like this. She believes that it made the classroom a bad learning environment. Since the teacher was so angry with the majority of the class, she only taught a few students. This student felt that was unfair because she wanted to learn, yet the teacher would not accept an apology. The student also felt that this happened because the teacher lacked any real control over the class.

Example: A teacher asked students to analyze a poem and write an essay on what they thought the poem meant. When the students received their essays, they noticed that those who interpreted the poem in the way that the teacher understood it received higher grades.

Student's Interpretation: Students felt that she did not follow the grading rubric because the essay's grade was only determined on the analysis rather than on writing skills. Even the students who had received a good grade felt that this was unfair. When a student asked the teacher why she had done this, the teacher said that she knew what the author had intended. Students felt that this was absurd because the teacher had not spoken to the author.

Example: A ninth grade student felt uncomfortable when the teacher sat on the desk directly in front of her.

Student's Interpretation: She felt that the teacher was too close and it was an inappropriate way for the teacher to instruct a lesson. It made the student feel self-conscious because she felt as though the teacher was focusing on her. Also she felt that the students in the room were also staring at her. However, she did not say anything to the teacher because she did not want to start problems. This student described herself as a very non-confrontational person.

My eleventh grade English teacher asked us to voice our opinion about Lenny's death in <u>Of Mice and Men</u> by George Steinbeck. I felt that George's action was justified for several reasons. When I explained my view to my teacher, she told me that I was wrong. She also believed that there was no way that I could have felt that way. I was outraged and screamed out that it was my opinion, and with the evidence I gave to support my view, there was no way that she could tell me how to feel. After several minutes of debating she still did not want to hear how I could possibly justify the killing of an innocent man.

Following September 11th, my teacher wanted to complete a project remembering the lives of those who died. It seemed like a nice idea, however we were asked to interview the victims' families only a few weeks after the tragic event. Many students, including myself felt that it was inappropriate to do this so soon after. I explained to my teacher that I would not be able to participate in this project and she threatened to fail me. I decided I would take a failing grade, and many other students had also decided to not do the project. She did not listen to why many students disagreed with certain aspects of this assignment and ultimately the students took it upon themselves to leave out parts that they determined to be intruding.

My interpretation: In both of these situations I felt that there was a miscommunication between the teacher and me. I think that if the teachers were able to listen to our views more, then we would be able to learn in an environment that we feel comfortable in. When my teacher told me I was wrong, I felt that if I did not agree with her then she would not respect me. However, this did not result in me agreeing with her. In fact it lead to many debates throughout the year. A less outspoken person might feel inclined to stay quiet when their views differ from the teacher. I also believe that it is not uncommon for teachers to not really listen to the feelings of students. Many people did not feel comfortable with the assignment, yet since the teacher thought it was a well thought out project, she did not want to listen to the opinions of others. I think that a major problem within the education system is a lack of listening. Teachers, parents, administrators, and students must all listen to the views of others and respect what they have to say, even if they do not agree with it all the time.

Mary Cate Cicero

Positive Communication between

High School Students and Teachers

Example: A student was having trouble in Math and the teacher was willing to help the student everyday after school in order to pass the test. When the teacher saw that the student struggled in Math, she thought of other options. After much thought, both the student and the teacher felt it would be best if the student took another class in order to receive credit.

Student's Interpretation: The student was very thankful that the teacher helped her with the material she was having problems with. It meant a lot to her that she was willing to not only take the time to help her, but also think of other solutions to the problem, and that they were both able to come up with a solution together through communication.

Example: A student was having a difficult time at home and it was showing through his schoolwork. The teacher called him into his office privately and told him that he knew he was a good kid, but was wondering why he had not been completing any of his work. Instead of getting angry with the student, the teacher wanted to find the problem and work towards a solution.

Student's Reaction: The student felt relieved to get a second chance in the class, and knew that he could go to someone when he needed help. It also showed that other people cared about his problems.

Example: One teacher always had the mentality to agree to disagree. He would listen to people's opinions, but then disagree if he felt otherwise.

Student's Reactions: The student felt that this opened the class for discussion and debates. She also felt that the teacher valued what everyone said and thought. She was not afraid to voice her opinion even if it differed from the teacher.

Elementary School Students

Example: A fifth grader was acting up at lunch by throwing trash at the neighboring house. The administrator punished the student by making him sit alone at lunch for the remainder of the year and asked the student not to return the next year. He accused the student of "starting a riot."

Student's Interpretation: The student felt that he was ostracized and did not feel as though his punishment was fair. He said that he had no intention of other kids joining in. This situation caused a lot of embarrassment and shame to the student, and did not mind that he could not return to school the next year.

Example: "It is taking all my strength not to lay my hands on you," a second grade teacher said to her students when they came in from lunch and were being loud. The students were quiet for a little while, but then continued to act out.

Student's Interpretation: They knew that the teacher was not going to hurt them and were frightened for a little while. The approach did not work because the students were not quiet for long. They had little respect for the teacher when she acted in this way.

Example: The English class teacher wanted the students to read the book <u>Treasure Island</u> aloud in class. One student really wanted to read, but was not called on. Instead the teacher called on an African American student and the other student sighed in disappointment. The teacher accused the student of being a racist, and she was forced to stand in the hall for the rest of the class.

Student's Interpretation: The student was mortified because the teacher thought that she was a racist when really she was only upset because she was not bale to read that class period. Since the student really liked the teacher and did not want her to think that, she spoke with the teacher after school and had everything cleared up.

Parents' Situations:

Example: A parent was called into a parent teacher conference because her child seemed to be shy. The parent explained that she was fine once she got to know people. The student then came in with a bruise from falling and the teacher sent the student to the nurse to be examined for the possibility of child abuse. However, the teacher did not ask the parent for permission.

Parents' Reaction: The parents became very angry with the teacher because there had been some sort of communication in the beginning that was ended when the teacher sent the student to the nurse. The parents could understand the teacher's concern, but thought there would have been a better way to go about this. They both felt that the teacher should have come to the parents before sending the student to the nurse. They were open with the teacher, however the teacher did not reciprocate the action. The parents felt that more communication would have been beneficial to their child.

Example: Two students had a physical fight in which a younger boy started the trouble. The older boy was trying to stick up for himself and never even touched the other boy. However, the teachers saw and gave them both detentions. The mother went to speak to the principal, but he would not listen. His excuse for giving the older boy detention was that he should have known better since he was two years older.

Parent's Interpretation: The mother felt that her son was being treated unfairly because he did not hurt the other boy. She felt that the principal was not able to "see the whole picture and did not take what she said into consideration." The punishment was not lessened and she still does not think this was a justified punishment.

Example: A teacher sent a letter home with one of her students because he was acting out in class. This student was known as a popular, yet outspoken child. This note was not flattering and failed to mention any of the student's positive contributions to class because he was normally attentive and smart.

Parent's Reaction: The mother felt that the teacher did not need to single her son out. He was acting appropriate for a thirteen year old boy. She felt that if there had been a real problem, the teacher should have spoken to the boy or the parent rather than just sending a note home. She felt that this was one way communication.

My Interpretation: When speaking to these students, I realized that many times they are confronted with situations that could have been avoided. Teachers do not realize how they make students feel with their words and actions. Though often times they offer many opportunities for students, the students can also become discouraged and uncomfortable when the teachers do not communicate in a constructive manner. Education should be a positive experience, and without the proper tools of communication, the true goals cannot be achieved.

WINNING STRATEGIES FOR CHANGE:

1. SEIZE THE OPPORTUNITY THAT CHANGE CAN BRING.

2. DON'T BE AFRAID TO TAKE A RISK

3. IT CAN'T BE DONE ALONE. WE NEED EACH OTHER.

4. IT TAKES TIME. BE PERSISTENT!

"Learn what you love, love what you learn: Clarifying Interest Based Learning in the classroom and the world."

When you're changing something, you're creating something new. **Here are the winning strategies for change:**

1. **Seize the opportunity that change can bring.**
2. **Don't be afraid to risk.**
3. **It can't be done alone. We need each other.**
4. **It takes time. Be persistent.**

In our rapidly changing world these strategies are invaluable to any one who finds themselves lost in the flood of new ideas and remedies. This is especially true of educators, who are constantly barraged with new "solutions" to the problems we face in schools today and made to follow those "solutions" to the letter, for better or for worse. For our purposes here, these educators are the people we will be dealing with and my intent is to help them meet whatever new standards are set forth, without compromising their integrity as a teacher who wants the children to learn and not just pass the tests.

1. Seize the opportunity that change can bring.

Change is going to continue to happen all around you and if you're not willing to look at the positive possibilities that arise out of it, you will get stuck where you are and disgruntled at the stagnancy of it all. You will feel you don't have a choice, but you do. Choice lies in every action. Don't get bogged down in the fact that you have to change, choose to change for the better.

When you chose teaching as a career you were motivated to make a difference in children's lives. You had a commitment and a vision about how to accomplish your goal. You need to get back in touch with that motivation and be willing to share it with your colleagues and administrators regardless of how you think they may react. Together you can observe and question the opportunities that change can bring.

2. Don't be afraid to risk.

This may not be an easy thing for you to do. It definitely wasn't easy for me because I was not running my classroom in a traditional style. To make change work we often have to go out on a limb. My motivation and commitment, as I said before, was to get children involved in the design of their own education, to inspire them to love to learn. It was a risk to ask the children how they wanted to go about this and a risk to tell my principal that this is what I intended to do but in the end I did both successfully. If you're committed to the outcome, risks come easier; you're willing to do different things, not just do things a little differently.

3. It can't be done alone. We need each other.

Change doesn't exist in a vacuum. One cannot simply do their own thing without suffering the ramifications of his or her actions. I learned this the hard way when I was teaching. Some administrators didn't like my method and said things like, "I know what works so do it my way." Others, to their credit, created communities that shared and worked together towards a common goal, were willing to try new things. These individuals were models towards a way of thinking. They allowed me to interact with them as people instead of titles, something few had allowed me to do before then. This type of open communication is imperative to any successful venture into the Interest-Based Learning method or similar types of collaborative teaching. It helps to create a support structure that will be there in success and defeat, one that will set common goals and be committed and responsible to ensure that they happen.

4. It takes time. Be persistent.

One should not expect to successfully accomplish his or her goals over night. At the same time one should not expect to accomplish one's goals without working towards them. It takes a strong commitment to stay the course. Reflecting, evaluating, and acknowledging your accomplishments is a motivation for being persistent, and persistence is what allows us to succeed in time. If you really want it, don't quit. In the end you'll find that despite all the hurdles you had to overcome, the path was a pleasure to travel. Your project is complete when you know it's complete. Only then can you move on to the next stage.

Chapter 3

Recipes for Success

I once heard a teacher comment to her student teacher: "If you give children choices, they will be confused." This is one ingredient never to use in education. Choices are a vital part of life, something children have been making since the earliest stages of their development. This is why the arts are so important. They instill a sense of self-awareness and self-understanding, which in turn gives them a base from which to make future choices. The arts make the difference between a child with strong decision making skills that have been nurtured and allowed to grow, versus a child with weak ones. Even in everyday situations, the importance is evident.

Kids are placed in a situation where they must make decisions all the time. They say, "Can I have two cookies?" at the bakery and their parents say, "no, pick one." They either deliberate then choose one, or they throw a temper tantrum and wind up with no cookies. Children who can use the problem solving process, having had it fostered and reinforced in them, are able to make these kinds of basic decisions easily and go home happy. Ones who haven't learned this skill get angry when they can't choose, and go home unfulfilled.

This is one of the repercussions of a teacher stifling a child's creativity. Too much strictness and rigidity in the classroom, like too much salt in a soup, can turn a child off to learning altogether. The worst part is that it only takes one situation, one cup of salty soup, to put a bad taste in a child's mouth.

Beyond this, making inquiries and allowing children to react to these inquiries in a wholly self-expressive way allows teachers to get to know their students. If a master chef knows his chefs-in-training he/she will be able to trust them to make good food. The same holds true for a classroom. If a teacher has gotten to know his/her students through asking questions and giving them options, he/she will trust them to make good decisions and be able to guide them towards take their own initiative.

In the following pages you will find a collection of real recipes with tips for teachers, as well as recipes for the classroom. These recipes will demonstrate in detail how to adapt the winning strategies for change to your classroom. They will help put interest-based learning into practice and promote teaching with integrity.

Building Trust With a Class Newsletter

Teacher/Classroom Activity

Overall Purpose/Intention:

To build trust between the students, the parents, and the teacher. To share with the parents how the students are involved in the development of the classroom and the problem solving process.

Materials:

Computer or typewriter; anecdotal records of class activities and experiences

Directions:

Read through the notes about the class and discuss with the class which information will be included in the newsletter. Use the children to help you figure out what will be the focus of the newsletter. Remember, this is interest-based learning!

Try to make the entries personal by including quotes from the children and specific anecdotes from the class' day-to-day achievements. Include your teacher comments as well so the parents can see what the students have accomplished both academically and socially.

Xerox copies of the newsletter for each student to take home to his/her parents so they can see how the class operates.

Update the newsletter regularly to continually update parents with class' progress.

Discussion:

Ask the kids open-ended questions like:

What would you like your parents to know about what happened in our classroom today?

How can we let the parents know about the problems we faced and how we found solutions to those problems?

How many different ways can we make a newsletter?

Do you think that your parents might have any ideas that could help us?

Tell the kids that the newsletter will be sent home at least once a week.

Variations:

Remember, you can always make the newsletters by hand or let the kids type it themselves and illustrate it. Try to make the newsletter as personal as possible.

Many programs like Microsoft Publisher have Newsletter Templates already to go.

Building Trust With a Class Newsletter Recipe

To build trust between the students, the parents, and the teacher. To share with the parents how the students are involved in the development of the classroom and the problem solving process.

INGREDIENTS

- Computer or typewriter
- anecdotal records of class activities and experiences

PROCEDURE

1. Read through the notes about the class and discuss with the class which information will be included in the newsletter.

2. Use the children to help you figure out what will be the focus of the newsletter. Remember, this is interest-based learning!

3. Try to make the entries personal by including quotes from the children and specific anecdotes from the class' day-to-day achievements.

4. Include your teacher comments as well so the parents can see what the students have accomplished both academically and socially.

5. Xerox copies of the newsletter for each student to take home to his/her parents so they can see how the class operates.

6. Update the newsletter regularly to continually update parents with class' progress.

7. Ask the kids open-ended questions like:

What would you like your parents to know about what happened in our classroom today?

How can we let the parents know about the problems we faced and how we found solutions to those problems?

How many different ways can we make a newsletter?

Do you think that your parents might have any ideas that could help us?

8.   Tell the kids that the newsletter will be sent home at least once a week.

Variations:

Remember, you can always make the newsletters by hand or let the kids type it themselves and illustrate it. Try to make the newsletter as personal as possible.

Many programs like Microsoft Publisher have Newsletter Templates already to go.

"*We're not accustomed to recognizing the power of each other's ideas; it's easier to take flight.*"
-*Deborah Meier*

Inspirational Ideas for

<u>*Building Trust with a Class Newsletter Recipe*</u>

Creating children as partners is like creating restaurant partnerships.

How can we appreciate/value all children and all foods?

The repercussions of a teacher stifling a child's creativity: it takes one situation to put a bad taste in a child's mouth. Too much salt, like strictness.

If you know how to listen to children, you will know how to allow them to take the imitative. If a master chef knows his chefs-in-training, he or she will be able to trust them to make good food!

Creating a New Web of Relationships

Classroom Activity

Overall Purpose/Intention:

To demonstrate the interconnectedness between people and the simultaneous diversity of the individuals that make up a classroom. To build community between the children and the teacher and the families.

Materials:

Large ball of yarn or colorful string; one completed "I Appreciate" list per student

Directions:

Have the kids complete an "I Appreciate" List (discussed earlier) and form a circle in the center of the room.

Ask the kids who would be willing to share their "I Appreciate" List with the others. Give this person the ball of yarn and allow them to share whatever they want from their list and that it's their choice.

Tell the child to pick someone else from the circle and to throw the ball of yarn to them while still holding onto the beginning of the yarn.

Repeat the process until everyone--even the teacher!--has read their "I Appreciate" List and is holding a part of the yarn (now an intricate web).

Discussion:

Ask the kids open-ended questions like:

What does this formation we created look like?

How does this web connect us?

What happened when you shared your "I Appreciate" List?

What new things did you learn about each other?

Why is it fun to share and discover new things with others?

Let the kids know that the class and the curriculum will be interconnected like the web they created. Share with the kids that learning relies on interconnectedness.

Variations:

Consider making this activity a regular feature of the classroom and even at your parent meetings.

Use this activity as a summary or concluding activity at the end of the year and take a photograph of the resulting web; and send copies to the kids and their parents or include the photo in the newsletter.

Inspirational Ideas for
Relationship Web Recipe

Creating children as partners is like creating restaurant partnerships.

"Families don't often eat together. When they do eat together, they share feelings. Families care about each other, no matter what happens. It brings closeness and compassion, otherwise separation."

GIVE SOME EXAMPLES FOR OUR

"I APPRECIATE" LIST:

I appreciate: (examples)

- I appreciate being taken seriously.
- I appreciate being treated with respect.
- I appreciate when my english teacher takes time out of his schedule to help me.
- I appreciate a teacher saying "let me help you" instead of "you're beyond help"
- I appreciate being singled out for my successes and not my errors.
- I appreciate when you talk to me like a friend, make me feel comfortable talking to you.

I appreciate it when you don't stare or whisper about me because I am handicapped or "different" from others.

I appreciate it when sales people are nice to me and help me reach things I can't reach because of my dwarfism.

I appreciate people treating me like I have a good brain and something to offer to society -- because I am short doesn't mean my brain is missing!

GIVE SOME EXAMPLES FOR OUR

"I APPRECIATE" LIST:

I appreciate: (examples)

- I appreciate being taken seriously.
- I appreciate being treated with respect.
- I appreciate when my english teacher takes time out of his schedule to help me.
- I appreciate a teacher saying "let me help you" instead of "you're beyond help"
- I appreciate being singled out for my successes and not my errors.
- I appreciate when you talk to me like a friend, make me feel comfortable talking to you.

_____

_____

_____

_____

_____

_____

Involving the Parents: Planning a Meeting

Teacher Activity

Overall Purpose/Intention:

To encourage the parents to actively participate in their children's learning environment by planning a meeting.

Materials:

Refreshments; interest items

Directions:

Figure out which date (or optional dates) would be good for you to have a teacher/parent meeting.

Figure out where you would like to have the meeting (home, auditorium, library, restaurant, etc.) and secure the location's use.

Reproduce the letter at the bottom of this activity, making any changes that you feel are necessary, and send the letter home with every child.

As a follow up, you might want to call the parents to see how many will be able to come to the meeting, or to see if another date would be more convenient for everyone.

During the meeting, have refreshments available.

Make sure you listen to the parents to demonstrate to them that they are an important part of their child's learning.

Variations:

Consider having meetings every month and at different locations (e.g. parents' homes, restaurants, etc.). You could even meet some mornings and have "coffee meetings."

Sample Letter (Reproducible):

(Date)

Dear (Parents' Names and Child's name),

Children are willing to learn more about the things and events that interest them personally. Much of my work--especially at the beginning of the year--is to listen to clues to those interests. Sometimes the children don't know what those interests are or if they are important. So we have the exciting task if finding out together.

My job is to present the possibilities through guest speakers and visitors, going on trips, reading books, magazines and newspapers, as well as contacting governmental and community groups. During this process I listen to hear what is clicking and will continue to hold their interest. Once we have developed a focus, we begin to make connections--that involves the entire "finding out process" of listening, summarizing, reporting, recording, and sharing themselves as well as the information.

I asked the children to bring in anything that interested them into the classroom during the first week of school. Based on what I heard and saw, I did some simple research and selected some books that they could read themselves and others for me to read aloud. Ask your child to tell you about those books. Help me listen to where those interests lie. Your participation will make a difference.

Books are an integral part of this learning process. I want children to become readers who not only learn to read but also read to learn--and enjoy it. That enjoyment can be fostered and encouraged by you and me. Let's discuss that as well as what I hope to accomplish this year.

PLEASE COME TO A MEETING ON THURSDAY EVENING, SEPTEMBER 20TH, FROM 7 to 9 PM.

Bring questions and ideas to the meeting. And bring your child, as well! This is going to be quite a year.

Sincerely,

(Teacher's Name)

Inspirational Ideas for Involving the Parents Recipe

Loud discussions are a must in order to be able to go from "oh god" to "oh, good!"

A "Just Talking" recipe

When there is free flow of ideas where everyone is heard, they can come to an agreement about the choices to be made, and make a decision.

"Just Talking Recipe"

Being willing to share interests

Valuing yourself and other people's opinions

You can't get it wrong!

Learning new things

Creating new relationships

Deepening these relationships

My mission, as an educator, is to create a classroom where learning is a desire. This requires a team effort between parents, teacher and student. This is facilitated, partly, through an open mind and an attitude of appreciation displayed by the teacher.

What's a team? It's all about commitment. In a team, together you are reinventing and reinterpreting the means by which you reach your common goal.

"It's all about not being in the process for yourself, but being involved for the contribution you can make for the children." –Malcolm Brown, Parent

There's no mail order. You must come in person to visit the classroom.

Setting the Stage with the Parents

Teacher Activity

Overall Purpose/Intention:

To create a relationship with the parents that encourages open sharing and honesty and that sets the stage for building trust.

Materials:

Telephone; note pad; 3-ring binder

Directions:

Contact parents during the summer and ask if it is a good time to talk. Introduce yourself and tell the parents why you are calling:

Hi. I am going to be Joey's teacher next year. I am calling to get acquainted and to find out as much as I can about Joey's interests. And I want to use those interests in developing the classroom's structure so the children can master skills, knowledge and information through class projects.

Ask the parents open-ended questions and pay attention to their descriptions and interpretations of the children. Take notes about these observations and about your own reactions to the discussion.

What do you think your child likes to do?
What are some of his/her talents and abilities?
What are some activities they seem to dislike?
What motivates and inspires your child?
How would you describe your child's social relationships?
What are your goals for your child's education?

Thank the parent for their time and let them know that you will be keeping them informed throughout the year and that they should feel free to call you at home and to share any questions or concerns.

Organize the 3-ring binder into sections for each child. Begin each section with the initial notes gathered from your parent interview.

Inspirational Ideas for
<u>Setting the Stage with the Parents Recipe</u>

"I'm really welcome here, even if you don't
like what I have to say." – a parent

What does having a voice mean? Where and how should
it be heard? How can/do we learn from each other?

Communication is the point. What if restaurants
had menus that were taste and flavor specific?

A true dialogue is appreciating the value of looking
at issues and problems from the other side's point
of view. In a classroom, too many cooks DON'T
spoil the broth—They make it more interesting.

What is important is to create a bridge of
communications. Speak from your heart.

Setting the Stage
with the Students

Classroom Activity

Overall Purpose/Intention:

To create a relationship with the students that encourages open sharing and honesty and that sets the stage for building trust. To allow the students to completely express themselves. To begin team-building process.

Materials:

Various objects representing the children's interests; chalk and chalkboard or chart paper for taking notes; notes taken from telephone interviews with parents and/or children

Directions:

Have the class form a circle in the center of the room with each child holding one of the items of interest. Ask the class who would like to share their impressions of the item they are holding. Or, ask the kids to pick a partner and for the partners to share their impressions of the various items.

To practice listening skills, ask the kids to repeat what they hear the others say about the items. Encourage every student to participate but don't force them.

Invite the kids to take a few minutes to share what questions they have about the various objects. Have a "classroom recorder" write down the questions--or record them yourself--on the board or the chart paper.

Tell the kids to think about how the class can explore these questions and find answers. Make a list on the board of the various resources that can be used in investigating the topics: museums, libraries, field trips, expert speakers, etc.

Tell the kids that time will be set aside everyday to share what is being accomplished in the inquiry process.

Developing Interests Through Interest Charts

Teacher/Classroom Activity

Overall Purpose/Intention:

To encourage the children to discuss what interests them and to make connections between those interests in order for teams to be formed and projects developed.

Materials:

Chart paper; chalk and chalk board; items the children have brought in reflecting their interests

Directions:

Discuss with the kids what their interests are and record these on a piece of chart paper or on the chalk board--or let a "class recorder" jot down the interests.

Discuss with the kids which interests go together; make another chart grouping connected interests.

Based on this second chart, invite the kids to form teams to explore similar or connected interests and questions they have about those interests and which kinds of projects each team might consider doing to fully explore their interests. Eventually, ask each group to choose a project they can work on throughout the year.

Ask each group to share with the class what are their interests and project-ideas.

Research possible information resources for the different groups' project ideas and interests. Share your discoveries with the groups: consider organizing field trips and/or guest speakers.

Note: Because this process is an evolving and emerging one, it can be adapted for various tasks throughout the year.

Discussion:

Whenever groups are given time to meet, use the interest charts to discuss such questions as:

Why do you think I am writing down everybody's interests?

How can these charts be used to discover connected themes and ideas?

What are some interesting things we could do as a class to research our interests?

What are some large topics that encompass all of our interests?

How can working in teams help you find solutions to problems or to better research interests?

Let the kids know that everyone can contribute to the process of learning; share with the kids how working together can frequently aid in the discovery process of learning.

Variations:

Consider using interest charts in administrative and teacher meetings to brainstorm school concerns.

Inspirational Ideas for
Developing Interests Through Interest Charts Recipe

Why are we so afraid of student's input in all aspects of school change?

"Kids say, "can I have two cookies?" And parents say, "no, pick one." They either deliberate and choose one, or they throw a temper tantrum. Children who use the problem solving process can chose, or get angry when they don't know how to make a decision." – Kate

Classroom as kitchen: children shape their education like deciding their own recipe-smooth, spicy, or crunchy. A Master Chef's recipe. A Master Chef asking the children must make a habit out of it. Train the students to be masters of what they want to do.

How do we take the passion and go beyond the requirements?
What would you do if they said, "go do it"
and you could do what you want?

If you know how to listen to children, you will know how to allow them to take the initiative. If a master chef knows his chefs in training, he or she will be able to trust them to make good food!

Create a self-discovery environment in the
classroom as well as in the kitchen.

What are your guiding principles? Winning principles to practice:
1. Give your children choices
2. Ask children what they are interested in
3. Find out who they are

4. Let children choose
5. Show an interest in the children's interests.

    When these principles are present, learning is present.

It's the children who will try new things – they show willingness that adults are more reluctant to show.

Former students have told me that they know when to be fully self-expressed… and when they had better shut up. Sometimes it had happened in High School, and more often in college.

Let's mess with the structures!

Inspirational Ideas for

Sharing Feelings Through Drama Recipe

Traditions that work will survive. The inquiry process is a tradition mostly with older students; let the younger students have a taste.

The repercussions of a teacher stifling a child's creativity: it takes one situation to put a bad taste in a child's mouth. Too much salt, like strictness.

Nurture the creative juices. Hunger in the classroom for knowledge.

I think and I write (or I write and I think!).

Arts in education could be the main dish, the spices, or the seasoning.

"The arts give children self-awareness, which gives them a base from which they can make choices." —Inez, art teacher

Little voices – big ideas

Fast food – not always good for you when you have too much and don't eat vegetables. Likewise, worksheets are not always good for you when they take away the appetite for investigation! Insatiable appetite for education comes from the "just talking" recipe and "just doing" recipe.

Sharing Feelings and Enhancing Communication through Read-Alouds

Classroom Activity

Overall Purpose/Intention:

To encourage the children to share feelings and to explore how emotions are expressed by analysing literary characters.

Materials:

Children's books (if possible pick out books related to the children's interests); dictionaries/thesauruses; art materials, such as paint and banner paper, charcoal and construction paper, etc.

Directions:

Regularly read aloud to the kids from books involving topics the students have expressed interest in.

As you read, discuss the various emotions experienced by the story's characters.

Have a "class recorder" take notes on the chalk board listing all of the various emotions recognized by the class.

After the read-aloud, have the kids look up new words in the thesauruses and/or dictionaries to further discuss the book's characters and their emotional states. Discuss with the kids how some words describe emotions while others both describe and evoke emotions.

Using the art materials, have the children make a colorful chart comparing different emotional states and also the subtle differences between words that deal with emotions; for example, happy vs. sad, sad vs. depressed, elated vs. chippy, etc.

Hang up the chart so that the children will have access to the emotional vocabulary it offers, and regularly add to it throughout the year.

Everyday, ask different children individually how they are feeling and to use new words from the chart to discuss their emotional states, if they choose too.

Discussion:

Ask the kids open-ended questions like:

Why is it important to share our feelings and identify our emotions?

What happens when we share our emotions with each other?

How do different words affect the story?

How do different words affect you?

What would happen to a story if we changed the adjectives describing the characters' feelings and emotions?

Let the kids know that there are many ways to communicate emotions and that they should feel open to sharing their feelings with each other--especially in the classroom and at home!

Variations:

Consider asking the children to rewrite the stories using new vocabulary words to see just how the stories are changed.

Sharing Feelings
Through Journals

Classroom Activity

Overall Purpose/Intention:

To encourage the children to share feelings and to explore how emotions are expressed by writing journals.

Materials:

notebooks or spirals books for each child; pens or pencils or crayons.

Directions:

Invite the children to keep a record of their thoughts and feelings of what is happening in the classroom or outside in other areas of their lives.

Encourage them to draw in addition to writing in order to describe their emotions on a given day.

Every day, ask the kids to share with the class from their journals and lead discussions about feelings and the difficulty in communicating emotions.

Encourage the kids to write in their journals about their progress in the class and about the new skills they are learning and mastering.

Try to develop activities that can involve the journal as much as possible.

Discussion:

Regularly ask the kids open-ended questions like:

Why does keeping a journal help you discover how you are feeling at different times.

Why do different people write such different things in their journals?

What did it feel like when you wrote down your feelings in your journal?

What did it feel like when you shared your journal with the class?

How could journals help us deal with our emotions in other places besides school?

Variations:

Set aside time each day for the journals; you can call it "Journal Time."

Make a collection of journal entries from the class: drawings, poetry, thoughts, tidbits, etc. Give each child a copy.

Write stories based on entries from the journals.

Keep a "Teacher Journal" about the class' progress and about each student's progress as well. Let the kids see you doing this to encourage them to write in their own journals.

In your Teacher Journal, include a section about different teaching strategies that work and those that don't with suggestions for improvement in the future. (I called my journal "Lessons I Learned" and regularly wrote in it about which approaches worked and what was missing that could be tried out or put in place).

"Unfolding": Growing Bean/Sunflower Plants

Classroom Activity

Overall Purpose/Intention:

To demonstrate to the class how each student is in the process of growing, like a plant; to demonstrate the concept of "unfolding" using a biological model.

Materials:

bean seeds (not food beans, which are treated to resist sprouting) for every child or team; soil; Styrofoam cups for every child or team

Directions:

Give each group or each child a Styrofoam cup and have them label the cup with their name/names.

Explain to the children that they will be planting and growing bean plants.

Next, give each child or group seeds and soil to place in their labeled cup.

Have the kids push the seeds into the soil in the cup and place each cup somewhere near a window.

The plants should begin sprouting in two to three days--water the plants once a week or so.

Have the kids take notes every day to describe the growth of their plants.

Discussion:

Ask the kids open-ended questions like:

How does the plant reflect what happens in a classroom?

Why is it important to take care of the plants?

Are all of the plants growing at the same rate? Why?

How are the plants like students?

In what ways does the plant "unfold"?

In what ways do the students?

Variations:

Consider integrating math into the activity by having the kids make charts showing the plants' growth over time.

Consider integrating reading/research practice into the activity by taking a trip to the library to look up books about plants and taking care of plants.

Inspirational Ideas for "Unfolding": Growing Sunflower Plants Recipe

Take each new piece that works and trust your heart to make a new piece to have the natural process. –Russian students.

"Planting in the Garden"
I try to plant more different kinds of vegetables than I can. I enjoy doing it; I enjoy seeing it grow. I enjoy eating it because I know that it's fresh from my garden. It's hard work to do, but if you enjoy it, it becomes easy. I grow different kinds of fruit, pears, plums, peaches, strawberries, raspberries; and you grow natural without chemicals. I don't spray or poison it.
- Jimmy's recipe

Plants that come back every year:
Oregano
Sage
Mint
Dill
They are not killed by the cold weather.
- Lina

"Unfolding":
Using Poetry to Recognize Growth

Classroom Activity

Overall Purpose/Intention:

To recognize how the class and the students have grown and "unfolded" by using creative poetry.

Materials:

paper and writing materials; examples of poetry (e.g. Shel Silverstein, haiku samples); construction paper and art materials

Directions:

Read examples of different poetic forms to the kids and discuss what messages the poet conveys through language.

Explain to the children that they will create their own poetry to discuss what they have learned by being a part of a classroom.

Ask the kids to write down ways they have grown; also, have the kids make notes about the different skills and facts that they have learned.

Next, using the examples discussed in class and the kids' notes, have the students create their own poetry about the ways they have grown and "unfolded,"

Ask the kids to share their poetry with the class.

Ask each kid to pick out their favorite poem; make a class anthology together using construction paper and art materials or even a computer publishing program.

Place the anthology in a display window for all of the school to see.

Discussion:

Ask the kids open-ended question like:

What thinking skills do poets use to write poetry?

Why are there so many different types of poetry in the world?

What does this tell you about the world's people?

How can writing poetry contribute to your creativity?

How does creating an anthology of work reflect how the class operates?

What lessons for life can we learn from reading and writing poetry?

How is the act of creating a poem similar to "unfolding"?

Variations:

Consider Xeroxing copies of the anthology for every student.

Consider making a student library in one corner of the room comprised of only student-centered works.

Inspirational Ideas for Using Poetry to Recognize Growth Recipe

Traditions that work will survive. The inquiry process is a tradition mostly with older students; let the younger students have a taste.

The repercussions of a teacher stifling a child's creativity: it takes one situation to put a bad taste in a child's mouth. Too much salt, like strictness.

Nurture the creative juices. Hunger in the classroom for knowledge.

I think and I write (or I write and I think!).

Arts in education could be the main dish, the spices, or the seasoning.

"The arts give children self-awareness, which gives them a base from which they can make choices." –Inez, art teacher

Little voices – big ideas

Fast food – not always good for you when you have too much and don't eat vegetables. Likewise, worksheets are not always good for you when they take away the appetite for investigation! Insatiable appetite for education comes from the "just talking" recipe and "just doing" recipe.

Developing A Central Theme

Teacher/Classroom Activity

Overall Purpose/Intention:

To have the students make connections between interests and agree upon a central theme that will be researched and explored throughout the year.

Materials:

Chalk and chalk board; old interest charts

Directions:

Tape the old interest charts you filled out with the class (or make a list of the students' interests on the board or on chart paper).

By now the kids have already formed teams to explore their similar interests. Ask the kids while sitting in their teams to discuss as a group how other teams' interests could be related to their own. Ask the teams to make a list of these "bridges."

Write down all of these "bridges" or "connections" on the board or chart paper.

Now ask the kids to consider one over-arching theme that would somehow tie-together all of the other team projects.

Write down all of these category ideas on the board.

Take a class trip to the library to research which of the categories would be most feasible while still offering interesting possibilities for research, projects, guest speakers, and field trips.

Agree on **one** theme that will become the year-long class topic of research.

Plan field trips and guest lecturers involving the agreed upon theme.

Agree on projects and itineraries dealing with theme.

Variations:

Create a display case of items representing the class theme and the teams' projects.

Inspirational Ideas for Developing a Central Theme

Why are we so afraid of student's input in all aspects of school change?

"Kids say, "can I have two cookies?" And parents say, "no, pick one."
They either deliberate and choose one, or they throw a temper
tantrum. Children who use the problem solving process can chose,
or get angry when they don't know how to make a decision." – Kate

Classroom as kitchen: children shape their education like deciding
their own recipe-smooth, spicy, or crunchy. A Master Chef's
recipe. A Master Chef asking the children must make a habit out
of it. Train the students to be masters of what they want to do.

How do we take the passion and go beyond the requirements?
What would you do if they said, "go do it"
and you could do what you want?

If you know how to listen to children, you will know how to allow
them to take the initiative. If a master chef knows his chefs in
training, he or she will be able to trust them to make good food!
Create a self-discovery environment in the
classroom as well as in the kitchen.

What are your guiding principles? Winning principles to practice:

6.   Give your children choices
7.   Ask children what they are interested in
8.   Find out who they are

9. Let children choose
10. Show an interest in the children's interests.

When these principles are present, learning is present.

It's the children who will try new things – they show willingness that adults are more reluctant to show.

Former students have told me that they know when to be fully self-expressed… and when they had better shut up. Sometimes it had happened in High School, and more often in college.

Let's mess with the structures!

Mapping the Curriculum: Making a Curriculum Tree

Teacher Activity

Overall Purpose/Intention:

To demonstrate to the class that the activities and projects they work on are connected to the state mandated curriculum.

Materials:

poster board; colors or markers

Directions:

Xerox the state mandated curriculum.

Cut out the standards in the shapes of leaves (you can even xerox the standards onto different colors of construction paper).

Next, repeat the above process with your lesson book, xeroxing the book, and cutting out the planned/completed activities in the shapes of roots. (Again, consider using colored construction paper to make the tree as spectacular as possible).

Draw a trunk of a tree with limbs labeled according to the various subject areas (math, reading, english, history, etc) and glue onto the poster board the "standards-leaves" corresponding to the appropriate "subject area-limb"; next, glue on the "lesson book-roots." (See example tree below)

Hang the tree up in the room where all the kids can see it.

As the year proceeds, continuing adding leaves and roots to the tree; and, regularly discuss with the kids how the tree is "growing."

Curriculum Diagram

Discussion:

Regularly ask the kids questions about the tree, like:

What does this tree diagram represent?

How is the tree similar to our classroom's structure?

What makes this tree continue to grow?

How does this tree reflect what happens in learning?

How does the tree illustrate what you have learned?

How can such a tree be used to show other connections in life?

Variations:

Consider having the kids build/glue the tree as a class activity.

Select a different student each week to "take care" of the tree by adding new roots(activities) and leaves(standards) to the posterboard using glue.

Plan Book Ideas: Connecting Projects with Curriculum

Teacher Activity

Overall Purpose/Intention:

To help the teacher organize their plan book in a way that facilitates interest based learning while still accomplishing the goals set forth by the mandated curriculum.

Materials:

blank teacher's plan book or lesson book; class roster

Directions:

Identify week's objectives and the days' objectives as you would regularly.

See which of the mandated curriculum could be covered while fulfilling your objectives for the week.

Next, go through the required texts and make a connection between texts, curriculum, and the kids' projects. Make sure you share with the kids which of the skills and curricula they are learning when studying texts or working in teams on projects.

Using your class roster, try to jot down notes for every child that will somehow include them in the week's activity; for example, "Johnny's poem used as example of haiku." Continue making notes and marking off each child until the entire class has been integrated into the weekly plan.

As the week proceeds, take notes in your plan book that describes whether various mandated curricula were met, which curricula needs to be recovered, kids who were not somehow integrated into the class plan, etc.

Variations:

Consider xeroxing your plan book from time to time and sending copies home to the parents so they can regularly see how all mandated curriculum is being met while projects are being explored.

Inspirational Ideas for Connecting Projects with Curriculum

Which actions would leave you unstoppable?

The arrangement of the classroom is like that of a restaurant: friendly, like a family, or aloof. Seasoned to taste: arts writing corners, activity centers, etc.

Spring and summer is production time. Preparation, presentation.

Skills at a glance—the skill, the description, the use, and the best example. Meatloaf, texture, substitution (the way we like it). Add unusual ingredients to taste. Iced coffee: real sugar or a sweetening substitute? Secret ingredients…

Storage: freeze completed project for later use (college resume). We should hold on to the kid's projects throughout the grades… portfolios.

If we have a four-star restaurant, can we have a four-star classroom?

Chronology of significant educational events, from schools in Westchester, Putnam, and New York City public schools. Like Culinary institutes- have they changed, or are they still churning out the same old recipes?

How hungry are you for reform?

"The smell of success"

"The smell of good education" – you can tell how good it is just from the aroma.

There are many points to get to – the important part is how we got through the transitions.

Start a question/observation journal: Tips for chefs and teachers.

"Success should be celebrated with French-fried onion rings and ice cream sundaes."

Let the decision holders meet and make some mistakes.

What if schools had curriculum choices: basic subjects, experiential, or a combination of both in the same school, where teachers chose the program and they all shared what they were learning so as to adapt to different ideas.

How can we tweak a recipe in the classroom as well as the kitchen?

Connecting and Summarizing with "Time Management Sheets"

Teacher/Classroom Activity

Overall Purpose/Intention:

To encourage the children to see that what they are learning each day is connected to every days' activities; and, to show the kids that they can manage their time effectively to achieve immediate and long-term goals.

Materials:

Copies of Time Management Chart for every student; pens or pencils; 3-ring binder

Directions:

Discuss with the kids that they will be filling out Time Management Charts every day in order to recognize how connected the lessons are and to summarize what was accomplished each day.

Pass out copies of the worksheets to every student and ask them to briefly fill out the worksheets.

Ask the class who would like to share the information they have written down on the worksheets. Let it be their choice.

Save select worksheets in the 3-ring binder as proof of children's growth and development. (You can share these with parents).

At the end of every day, use the worksheets to summarize what was accomplished and which skills were practiced and/or mastered.

Let the kids know that these forms will be distributed almost everyday as a summarizing activity.

Note: See reproducible worksheets at below.

Discussion:

Ask the kids open-ended questions like:

Why do you think we fill out these forms everyday?

How can these forms help us see how every lesson is connected?

How can these forms be used to track our growth and progress throughout the year?

How might these forms be adapted for use in other areas of our lives besides school?

Variations:

Change the form by adding/modifying the questions.

You can even keep folders of each child with their Time Management Sheets in order by date as a progress track.

Inspirational Ideas for Time Management Sheets Recipe

Certain recipes require certain procedures, tools, ingredients… the same goes with education.

"But you have to do your homework." The tone of her voice was nasty and angry. I came over to look and she said, "don't look over his shoulder; it'll distract him." It was a history lesson. Why couldn't I say anything? It was a Supreme Court lesson, and she said, "you've got to do all the courts." She pressured him, not asking him questions, but just telling him what to do. "Is this the only homework you've got for social studies?" She then asked. But what else can a parent say? An example of a master chef bossing the other chefs around: do it MY way.

Joan – Roast Duckling Recipe

Very often we look at a project and it seems daunting. If we analize it many times, we can find a way to simplify our effort to make it manageable. For example, in experience cooks might hesitate to undertake roasting a duck. They're afraid it would be fatty, or undercooked or overcooked. But if you take that duck and quarter it before you cook, it simplifies the cooking process and the end results are foolproof.

1. Duck cut in quarters
2. Season with: salt, pepper, garlic powder, onion powder
3. Place skin side up, in roasting pan
4. Cook 1 hour at 350 degrees
5. Remove fat (pour off)
6. Return to oven one hour more

Sauce

1. Jar of orange marmelade
2. 2 tbls. White vinegar
3. 2 tbls. Brown sugar
4. Heat in sauce pan
5. Spread sauce over duck and reheat ½ hour at 325 degrees

Tips for Teachers

If the project seems too difficult break it down into segments.

It's Your Choice: An Exercise in Critical Thinking

A Classroom Activity

Overall Purpose/Intention:

To give students repeated opportunities to experience the power of focused, critical thinking; to demonstrate the many possible opportunities/paths for each respective dilemma or goal; to encourage creativity.

Materials:

Timer or clock/watch with a second hand; chalkboard and chalk; a list of topics (see below) written on the board or a chart prior to the session; writing materials for the recorder of each small group.

Directions:

Tell the students that you need their help in doing some critical thinking.

Ask the students if they know what *brainstorming* is. Listen to the comments of those who have participated in brainstorming sessions before, and clarify that brainstorming is a process in which many ideas or options are generated for solving a problem or handling a situation. In your own words, explain further, using an example:

Imagine that you and a friend want to surprise another friend by doing something special on his or her birthday. There are many possible things that you could do, but until you discuss your ideas with others and think about your options, you can't make a choice. The more ideas you come up with, the better your chances of choosing the perfect surprise. You decide to hold a brainstorming session and spend five minutes listing as many ideas as you can think of. You write them all down, not stopping to discuss any of them until the five minutes are up. Just keep thinking and throwing out ideas. Afterwards, go back and talk about each idea, and then agree on the best one.

Ask the students if they can help you make a list of rules for brainstorming, based on the process you just described. You should end of with these rules on the board:

1. Suggest as many ideas as you can think of. Don't worry about details, just be creative.
2. Write down every idea.
3. Don't reject, put down, evaluate or discuss any idea during the brainstorming process.

Have the students form small groups of four or five and choose a recorder. Make sure that the recorders have paper and pencils. Then, in your own words, explain the assignment:

Pick a topic from the list I have prepared. I will give you the signal to start brainstorming. You will have 3 minutes to come up with as many ideas as you can think of. Write them all down, and be sure to follow the rules. At the end of 3 minutes, I'll give you the signal to stop.

Circulate and observe the groups. Call time at the end of 3 minutes. Do a quick check of each group, commenting on the number of ideas generated, reinforcing the students for their creativity. Review any rules that the students had diffvculty with.

If possible, have the groups repeat the process several more times, using new topics during each round. Do not evaluate (or allow the students to evaluate) any suggested ideas. Focus entirely on gaining practice in brainstorming. Reserve about 10 minutes for a culminating class discussion.

Discussion:

Ask open-ended questions like:

What happened for you during the brainstorming process?

Why is it helpful to think of many different solutions to problems?

What could you do after you have a long list of ideas?

Why not just do the first thing that pops in your head?

Variations:

When working with younger students, conduct the brainstorming sessions with the total group. facilitating and writing ideas on the board.

Action Plan for Solving Problems

Classroom Activity

Overall Purpose/Intention:

The children will identify simple strategies used in solving problems and making decisions.

Materials:

a copy of the "Action Plan for Solving Problems" worksheet; a pencil for each child

Directions:

Introduce the activity: Explain to the children that they can solve many problems by following a few easy steps. Describe a theoretical dilemma that you might have, such as: *Why are my houseplants turning yellow and dying?* Model the worksheet by following the steps in the template and writing them on the board.

Describe the dilemma in as much detail as possible. For example: "The leaves on my houseplants started to turn yellow a month ago when we had such hot, dry weather. Even though I watered the plants every day, the leaves got yellower until the plants began to die."

List the possible opportunities created as a result of this dilemma: "I could 1) look in a book about plants to learn about plant care and diseases; 2) ask a friend for advice; 3) call a plant store or nursery and describe the problem; or 4) throw out the plants and start over."

As an example, choose one option that sounds the best for you. "I asked a friend, and she suggested to give my plants more water. The plants died. I wonder if I gave them too much water? I'm still thinking about what else I can do."

Ask the children their advice on what is possible that you didn't think of.

"What other options do I have, that I can test out?"

After the children have helped you with your theoretical dilemma, ask them to think of one that *they* might have. Follow the Action Plan once more, with their help. Again, record your actions on the board.

Discussion:

Acknowledge the children for their problem-solving skills. Ask them:

- *Why is it important to know how to solve problems?*
- *How do you think this skill might help you in school? In a job when you are an adult? In your personal relationships?*

Variations:

Ask the children to think of (and solve) a problem with a partner. Distribute copies of the "Action Plan for Solving Problems," and ask the partners to fill out the steps. Walk around the room and offer assistance as needed. Invite the children to share their completed Action Plans with the class.

Ask the children what problems they are faced with in regard to their team projects and if they see any possible solutions. Open the dialogue to other teams to see if anybody can offer any advice or support. Stress that everybody's opinions are important.

Set aside a time at least once a week for students and teachers to discuss any personal and/or academic issues they might have, and allow for non-judgmental listening. This type of listening allows children to make choices without the burdens of feeling that they are being judged. The teacher's role is to be the mentor for this type of ongoing dialogue, which encourages critical thinking and decision-making.

Building a "Thinking Skills Vocabulary"

Teacher/Classroom Activity

Overall Purpose/Intention:

To demonstrate to the kids that they are learning new skills and to help them identify those new skills using vocabulary they may not be familiar with..

Materials:

banner paper or construction paper; note cards; markers; copies of state standards

Directions:

Go through your state standards and make a list of "thinking skill" words like "infer, analyze, classify, summarize, etc."

Write the thinking words on the banner paper using magic markers (or have the kids write/paint the words as an activity while you define what the words mean and offer examples).

Hang the banner paper on the wall where the kids can see the words; or, if you choose to write the words on notecards, hang the cards all over the room and/or from the ceiling.

Everytime the kids use one of the thinking skills identified, refer to the corresponding thinking skill word on the banner paper or notecard.

Try to encourage the kids to use the vocabulary whenever they are performing the thinking skill involved.

Discussion:

Regularly ask the kids open ended questions like:

Do all thinking skills require the same energy or focus?

How are thinking skills alike and different?

How can thinking skills help you in your day-to-day life, like jobs and school and home?

How might thinking skills help artists? Scientists? Teachers? Students?

How could we practice using the thinking skills more often?

Variations:

Consider laminating the notecards or the banner paper so that they can be reused the following years.

Make up a worksheet with all of the thinking skills in columns and make copies for every child. Every day encourage the kids to check off the thinking skills as they use them. You can make this a game of sorts. Save these worksheets for every child so their parents can see how the kids' thinking skills are being incorporated into the lessons.

Take notes in your plan book of the kids' progress with the thinking skills.

Creating a True Dialogue Recipe

Overall Purpose/ Intention:

To encourage the parents to actively participate in their children's learning environment by planning a meeting.

Ingredients:

Xeroxed "I Appreciate" List for each student; pens or pencils

Procedure:

Tell the kids that they are going to create appreciation lists of specific accomplishments and to chare their lists if they choose to

Hand out worksheets to the kids and walk around and offer support.

Ask the kids if anyone would be willing to share what they have written down. Make sure they every student who shares feels supported and not judged.

Ask kids open-minded questions like:

Why is it important to acknowledge out accomplishments?

Why is it important to recognize accomplishments even outside the classroom?

How should we react when others share their accomplishments with the class?

Tell the kids that at the end of each day, time will be set aside for appreciating what was accomplished both individually and as a whole group.

Variations:

Send copies of "I appreciate" Lists home with the students for their parents to fill out.

Opening the Door to Full Self-Expression and Participation

Classroom Activity

Overall Purpose/Intention:

To show the students ways they communicate and how others interpret their facial expressions and body language.

Materials:

Pictures from magazines or personal photographs showing people with various emotions; chalk and chalkboard

Directions:

Again, have the class form a circle in the center of the room. Pass out the pictures or photographs to the students.

Invite the kids to examine the emotions of the people in the pictures and to describe how they think the people are feeling and why.

Ask a child to try and mimic the people's expressions and emotions using their own facial expressions and body language. Let the other kids guess what emotion the person in the picture is expressing based on the student's interpretation.

Ask the children to think of as many emotions as they can and then write the corresponding words on the board so they will have access to descriptive vocabulary. Add your own words if they are not on the list, for example:

surprise	curiosity	anger
boredom	confusion	fear
disgust	joy	shyness
sadness	sympathy	disappointment

Have the children agree on a word that most closely describes the emotion being conveyed.

Repeat the process for all of the children willing to participate.

Have the kids gather in one area to discuss the activity.

Discussion:

Ask the kids open-ended questions like:

What do these words make you think about?

How do facial expression and body language contribute to our communication?

What makes these expressions occur?

Do we have control over our expressions?

Share your own thoughts about emotions and how they are communicated through facial expressions and body language.

Variations:

Use pantomime to act out a story or have the kids act out a familiar story using just their body language without spoken words or props. For example:

The window is stuck. Try to open the window. (Pull. Strain. Bend your knees.)

You are at a playground and you are going too fast down a slide or on a swing.

Inspirational Ideas for Opening the Door to Full Self-Expression Recipe

What if we said "you can't get anything wrong?"

"Families don't often eat together. When they do eat together, they share feelings. Families care about each other, no matter what happens. It brings closeness and compassion, otherwise separation."

When I am expressive, it causes other people to be expressive.

It's the children who will try new things – they show willingness that adults are more reluctant to show.

How do we take the passion and go beyond the requirements? What would you do if they said, "go do it" and you could do what you want?

How do recipes last for centuries? What makes new ideas interesting for teachers? Bring in "cooks" who have tried it. And you've got to taste it, not just try it.

A Recipe For Success In Public Schools

1) Ongoing relationship building is imperative in creating a climate for sharing.

2) In Interest Based Learning Schools every child, every parent and every teacher listens and hears "one another" with understanding, empathy and respect.

3) In order to create a team, there has to be a willingness to be a team.

4) What if every child and every parent said, "I am really welcomed here. I can walk in, and they are really glad to see me."

5) What a teacher should be: Someone who says, "We must let the children teach us how to help them successfully meet the new standards of in education."

6) Why aren't we asking the children?

7) Bureaucracy: someone telling you what to do and what not to do.

8) What would it take to make asking the children a habit?

9) If we want involved, informed citizens, let's have involved, informed students.

10) Every article and news story written about children in schools will include a child's voice.

11) Teacher applications should be judged by the three H's: head, heart, and chutzpah.

12) What are the questions we should be asking for the answers we already have?

13) How can a student be proficient in the skills, knowledge, and information needed for life? The point is to create, and it takes time to create.

14) It's the process that creates the habits that are practiced, not the products. So what are the habits that we want children and families to practice, and what is the process that will lead to those habits? Ask the children.

15) Every person makes a choice when they do something. People don't really understand that it *is* their choice.

ELAINE'S BIO

An educator with over thirty years of elementary classroom experience, professor at several universities, teacher trainer, speaker, mentor, workshop designer and leader, and educational consultant, Elaine Young tirelessly has examined the classroom experience from all angles. Based on her experience working with many diverse populations, including migrant students, children of working parents and children in affluent communities, Elaine created the Interest Based Learning model to train future teachers and assist current educators in creating high interest classrooms with motivating strategies and activities that involve all students working with the adults in the problem-solving process and building collaborative teams who are all learners together that can make a difference. This method shifts the emphasis away from traditionally structured standardized learning and focuses the curriculum around students' interests and needs, inspiring their desire to learn and a new dedication to their work.

Through this shift, Elaine was able to introduce new and exciting ways of having the students master core material on a daily basis. A partnership with parents, teachers and students for learning is formed using this model, creating a new level of respect and communication in the class environment.

Author of two previous books (*I Am a Blade of Grass* and *Creating a High Interest Classroom*), Elaine Young has also authored a screen play called Flyer, describing the actual obstacles and conflicts she faced in her own journey as a radical classroom teacher who wanted to improve the classroom experience of her students, and how she overcame the barriers to change.

Elaine, who holds a B.A. in Elementary Education from Queens College and a M.S. and Permanent Certificate / Supervisor of Elementary

Education from the State University of New York at New Paltz, continues to advocate and teach about the importance of giving the children a voice in all important education issues. She believes if we want a world where we value, appreciate and cherish everybody's children, then we must involve the children in creating that world.

Printed in the United States
128821LV00005B/274/P